MY SECOND LIFE

DEEPAK KUMAR GUPTA

Made with ♥ on the Notion Press Platform
www.notionpress.com

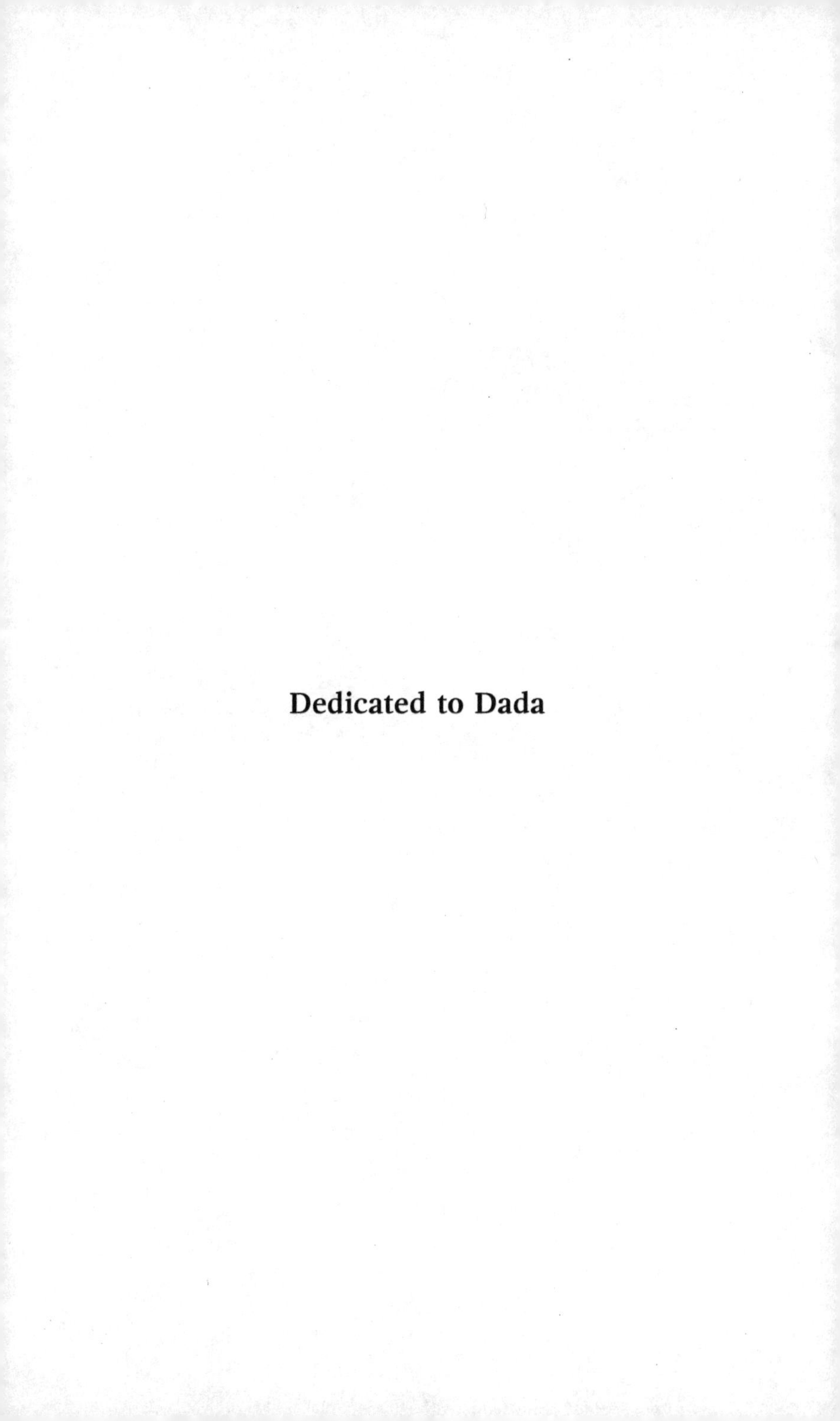

Dedicated to Dada

Contents

Foreword

My relationship with Gupta.

My acquaintance with Mr. Gupta started in the 1990s. Being a decade younger than I, his savviness always influenced me. It was he who advised me on a proper dress sense while taking my daughter to her first rock concert. Our closeness increased that he shared some of the fretting over a cancer in his eyebrow with me. Admittedly, I remember nothing of the pimples on his ass. An abrupt loss of touch for a score of years culminated when I met him serendipitously September 2023 for a retreat. He appeared as fit as a fiddle. As a befitting celebration of our reunion, he bestowed on me the honour of writing a foreword to a book he intended to publish. Not surprisingly, September 18, 2023 was the most recent and final entry in the book.

How Mr. Gupta's work affected me positively.

As I followed the sequentially dated narrative entries of Mr. Gupta's struggle to restore health, I could sense his level of resilience. The persistence and determination described in this book resonated with me as Mr. Gupta has clearly reconciled to his compromised state of health. It is highly cathartic to read the line "my life is going to be – fantastic." as the latest entry in his diary.

My opinion of the book and its theme.

A unique blend of in-depth suggestions and an autobiographical diary-type account of Mr. Gupta's discoveries was truly refreshing and effective. By suggesting pragmatic benefits instead of firm recommendations, readers will find these ideas easily applicable. A chronological recount of the discoveries facilitates the reader to personally apply the results in a self-exploratory way. An isolated experimenting has been done with an equal importance given to others. Although the discoveries are described as those of the author, Mr. Gupta includes the involvement of his ex-wife, the massage, suntan parlour girl, the chatroom girl and Scanty Panty. The author without qualms shares with others the results of his findings.

The book's historical impact.

It is too early to judge the impact of this book. One is tempted to compare Mr. Gupta's experiments to the miraculous discovery of Penicillin notatum by Dr Alexander Fleming.
Mr. Gupta refers to the well-known concept that stomach absorption deficiencies can be overcome by applying medications topically to the skin or injecting them. His discovery after 60 months of healing the stomach absorption deficiencies was that he could enjoy therapeutic benefits of drops of oil in his coffee.

Two additional observations.

October 27, 2018, Mr. Gupta mentions early 1900's Nobel prizes involving UV light. He adds that "overexposure meant certain fates unimaginable to mice and men at that time." "So I was very careful to follow Scanty's instructions". This reminded me of the skills with safety that Mr. Gupta demonstrated when he drove the bus of children.

I was aware of the uneasiness of the situation with Mr. Gupta's father and his brother. I did not realize the full impact of this until I read the entry made in October 2021, "I was the quintessential underachiever good for nothing from the outside and from the inside I felt my life was disposable until a few days ago really."

-- Philip Klemka
Practicing physician and psychotherapist

SECTION 1

CHAPTER I

The Big Lie

$2/Virus $12/Chronic

March 17, 2018

What do both men and women want – in common?? **Procreation and a better quality of life.**

THIS SECTION serves as a guide as to how to do the above.

The **NEXT SECTION** talks about **OBTAINING THAT BETTER QUALITY** and a **COMPLETELY HEALTHY AND PAIN FREE LIFE for $100.**

The **WHOLE** attempt is to prove that all areas of physical and social deviation, all "mental problems" are caused by long term chronic maladies of the physical body. All addictions are caused by physical inflammation – curing pain. What will my addictions levels be in say 3-4 years??

The indicators of the above will be sought by using both **Scanty Panty UltraSex 40 and 100 hour "activator" oils** with the same attitude – **JUST GO WITH THE FLOW.**

In other words – **I WON'T CHANGE ANYTHING DELIBERATELY.** What I want is **improvement** of **calcium phosphorous levels** in say - **2 weeks** and **betterx-ray results** of shadows and spots **from scarring** in around - **6 weeks.**

These are my notes as I go through the process below – but the main aim is to actually prove that this WHOLE IMPROVEMENT IN LIFE lies in the gastro intestinal tract and by obtaining perfect digestion I can achieve perfect metabolism - constitution – and immunity system – thereby saving the cost of exorbitant medical bills.

But remember the query about what will automatically crop up in relationship with mental issues. **Are ALL mental problems caused by physical malady??**

And in relationship to toxin use or abuse – and "sexual deviance" will there be a correlated desire to **stop purposely**?

Now we have indicators like THE **NEED FOR SPEED** being reduced on all levels. So with a body with perfect health can I maintain this without drinking the **OIL??** I could just bathe in it and ... will my drug desires lessen or naturally stop completely? And equally important –
IS ALL SICKNESS CAUSED BY CHEMICAL IMBALANCE CAUSED FROM POOR FOOD, MALNUTRITION AND ENERGY ABSORPTION?

Now remember the next books are about **ME AND NOT YOU** ingesting the SAME oil – bathing in the oil –

two months on – two weeks off for 50 weeks and then stopping to use the oil entirely - **I** make **MY** body strong enough to ... **YOUR DOCTOR CAN INJECT VITAMIN D USING ENCLOSED CITINGS OR THE INTERNET.**

THIS SECTION IS ABOUT USING THE 40 HR OIL ON THE OUTSIDE OF MY BODY

CHAPTER II

Miserable Immunity

April 4, 2018

Those pimples on my ass are anything but a source of comfort. Open wounds and handrails are carriers of about four hundred rounds of all the germs in the world – My terrible immunity system does not better the situation.

Fungus and the mighty bacteria and viruses scare the living daylights out of me. Bugs that bite germs that don't bite. If I calculated every contaminant that has entered my system. Just – living life.

I don't know how my ex wife could stand it. And those pimples on my butt.

So if I bring up %!@# *& Star now it's not because of her relaxed smile or her cute butt it's because she doesn't seem to run eight miles before hitting the gym. As far as BMIs and simple height weight age charts her body is exactly what I am shooting for. Effortless. Totally Fit.

Now this book is for couch potatoes. **I PLAN TO – REVERSE MY SYMPTOMS – ALL MY SYMPTOMS. IN REVERSE.** There is something I didn't mention yet - it's that I plan to **NOT** exert my heart until my symptoms - STOP. It is a part of the concept called convalescing but there is the point.

WITH SCANTY PANTYS CURE I SHOULD BE ABLE TO RECOVER AUTOMATICALLY WITHOUT CHANGING MY ENVIRONMENT OR ANY HABIT

So later I went on a visit to a filthy place where I shared whatever with whoever - This chatroom girl is showing me her ad shots for her self promotion. I saw pictures of her butt – and no pimples. I told her I was impressed.

She was free to talk about whatever I wanted. So I told her about my visit to the sun tan parlor.

She was ^@*&# me after I ^@*&# her three times. Everything but sex was the deal. With reference to my photos, I told her when it hurt and I lifted my head and first looked at her chest and then right into her eyes and said it aloud – **YOU HIT MY HITLER SPOT.**

I live in a protected environment which ironically neither acts as a shield nor enhances my immunity . The places I went to and the people I have shared bodily fluids with is an astronomical 42,000 in 14 months.

Health comes first and may be an ongoing process. To remove the old environment from our bodies. On a continuous basis. **EXCESS TOXINS.**

CHAPTER III

Reversal of Symptoms

Now I am being irresponsible for knowing this ... just being dumb for that butt looked good. Looks great. And will always look fantastic.

May 28, 2018

Though these books are about sex and physical perfection and the desire to breed, it is more about **REMOVING THE FEAR OF** and becoming impermeable to outside and inside infection.

Savouring sex is more fun than sex but there is usually only one person around. this is a book on health for couch potatoes like me.

WHOEVER YOU ARE IF YOU WANT OR NEED THESE ORGANS TO REPRODUCE.

Remember I started out this story about two beautiful women. That lady at the sun tan parlor was the **A PURE ANTONYM OF CHEAP** – she was gorgeous and made me feel good about myself - and my gal pal is a beautiful and seriously swashbuckling woman. That was 2 months ago and I was bragging boisterously that I got the biggest @#$&* – and can **%&#) 5 times a day** – using **Scanty Panty ^@*&# oil ...**

I inadvertently ran into another beautiful woman and I broached upon procreating with her.

All of a sudden everybody drifted away from just flirting just because of this conversation I brought up with my massage girl – to some very serious hardcore masturbation with these two women –

Scanty's main source of oil was an ultra violet light. 275 watts of power and a cage that came with it. She poured 3 liters of canola oil in a glass pitcher and beamed the light at close distance through the open top and left the light on for 2 days. She sent me a glass jar of the product and she had me bathe in about a tablespoon of oil once a day. "a quick pour" out of a glass.

She said – don't meddle with it. I could try using it on my guitars.

And then the accident happened. I was going to make love one night and my hand slipped into a jar of this 2-day oil. I mean this was meant for my guitars and had had it on my hands for months. And that's how it happened. My hands were healing from the use of the guitar oil and I thought ... GO FOR IT!!

Now this was before I found out about creating Vitamin D with ultraviolet light. It became what turned out to be the transfer of energy through air to create a chemical change in the oil. The radiation would become virtually ineffective after 17 hours.

CHAPTER IV

Revitalizing The Vitals

It was healing my hands – cleaning my guitars as we hit the 40 hr oil and oops – my hand automatically slipped – **DOWN THERE – BANG BANG – ROCKET SHIP.**

You can imagine spending the last 8 years in solitude and finding out everybody else is getting laid by 200 people while I lay dormant wondering if my 3000 times with someone I was married to as well as the three hookers really count. Now that I am awake I see nothingness. There is nothing here.

You can well comprehend the amount of hate that had built up. Everybody else not only had a life but also had a good time at it. I was looking for someone 8 years ago and they had their lives and I asked – is there anybody who can help me?? 10 minutes is all I need. My newly bought used flannel sheets looked fresh and unused. I needed to be cozy in winter. I didn't know I was going to make it through. The sheets were washed once in 8 years. I had ripped my arms through and lain on the bare mattress. It took a day to get absolutely comfortable with that little bit of disgrace. I have had the actually energy to wash the outside of my car with a spray gun twice in 2 years the carpet – none – I was looking for two extra hands for 10 minutes.

Nobody even remotely helped. My two best friends got laid 200 times while I just needed a little bit of help because I was a gimp. The fact is - all the dirt I have been living in has been gathering over 4-8 years.

It's not like I don't have any friends I just don't have any right now. I did have friends at a certain time in my life but no. I fear everything. I have actually never been touched by a person who really cared two hoots about me. In the last 8 years I had been laid once by the girl who took my photographs.

And loneliness hurts. People told me you get used to it but you never do. I have never asked anyone out on a romantic date or encouraged any friendship. I do not contact people.

Everybody is out to make a fast buck. Sitting at home I was looking for ways to kill time. I got really good at a few things. These girls could not spare ten minutes to make a bed for me and I had loads of time to have a good time. I lived in utter humiliation.

Help me with my own goals and maybe I could make some money to serve myself dough. Nope concerts and Toronto is all I ever heard about. So, killing time is what this book is all about. I extend this to Scanty Panty Sex and Solo oil for solo and conjugal fun. If you are a real go getter like me, it takes about 1.25 hrs. to whack 3 times a day. Now, I don't have a job and I have a lot of time on my hands but year by year I save a lot of hassles by living my life with no one.

CHAPTER V

Flying Solo

The solution – Solo Kama Sutra. **WITH SCANTY PANTY GO FOR 5. 5X IN 24 HRS.**

A Bikini Model with a hot body does not mean perfect health – maybe 80 percent max. – that I am sure is a major concern for every individual. Now there was the yoga class and the kids.

Why 3 times a day for men and women. During adolescence, everybody knows to be sex god the magic number is five. Now on a good day I can manage five and I am a dude. How about gushing the real messy stuff is the real deal.

USING SCANTY PANTY ON YOUR GENITALS AS WELL AS YOUR PARTNERS CAN MAKE YOU VERY FERTILE. IT IS A STERILIZER AS WELL AS HORMONE AND STEROID. IT WILL GET YOU GOING AND MAINTAIN YOU SO.

Remember ladies – I may be the biggest pimp. But I can be the best hooker when you want me to be. So, a solo act or with a partner or your partner is a gal or dude will make life more comfortable –there is health in sex acts that aid in getting your health – perfect.
Perfect health = PERFECT REPRODUCTION. FERTILITY. VIRILITY.

Reproduction is not funny. It is fear. The very ability defines our self esteem but ^@*&# is massage and massage is a medical application used to revitalize every organ in our bodies.

I wanted energy transfer but when that girl at the massage parlor tanning spa did mine as hard as she let me do hers -

SHE HIT A SPOT A HURT SPOT I ENDED UP CALLING THE –

HITLER SPOT.

THAT WAS ME. NOW HERE IS WHAT YOUR DOCTOR WOULD DO.

CHAPTER VI

Importance of Vitamin D

VITAMIN D (CALCIFEROL) DEFICIENCY (1) (Rickets; Osteomalacia)

At least 10 compounds have vitamin D activity, but only two have practical significance: ergocalciferol (activated ergosternol, vitamin D2), the chief form in viosterol, irradiated yeast, and “metabolized” or yeast milk; and cholecalciferol (activated 7-dehydrocholesterol, (vitamin D3), formed in human skin by sunlight or ultraviolet light and the chief form in fish oils, eggs, and irradiated milk. Each has been isolated in crystalline form.

Vitamin D functions in **normal bonemetabolism** by regulating the **intestinal absorption** of **calcium** and **phosphorous.** Vitamin D has recently been shown to be **essential for the synthesis of a protein that transports calcium across the mucosa**. D2 and D3 have been shown to exist is 25-hydroxy active forms in the body. When sufficient amounts of vitamin D, calcium and phosphorous are available in the diet, regardless of their ratio, blood serum values tend to be normal. The disturbance of calcium and phosphorous metabolism caused by vitamin D deficiency results in **rickets** and sometimes tetany in infants and children and **osteomalacia** in adults.

Daily dietary allowances are extremely variable, depending on the amount of vitamin D formed in the skin as a result of ultraviolet radiation and on the efficiency with which the body can metabolize calcium and phosphorous. (For recommended daily allowances.

Vitamin D deficiency follows inadequate exposure to ultraviolet rays, but under usual living conditions in temperate climates is due to inadequate intake. Conditioned deficiencies are caused by **malabsorption** (e.g., chronic steatorrhea) or by poor tissue utilization (refractory or vitamin D-resistant rickets).

Pathologic changes in children consist essentially of **defective calcification of growing bone** and hypertrophy of the epiphyseal cartilages. Epiphyseal cartilage cells cease to degenerate, but new cartilage continues to form, so that the epiphyseal cartilage becomes irregularly increased in width. In chronic deficiency, the cancellous bone of the diaphysis and of cortical bone may be resorbed.

After adequate treatment, degeneration of the cartilage cells within 24 hr and penetration by a vascular network within 48 hr permit calcium and phosphorous deposition. Osteoid material at the diaphysis ceases to form and normal endochrondal production of new bone is resumed. In adults, osteoid signs of deficiency are similarily reversed: cancellous bone and the diaphysis disappears and the cortical bone is resorbed.

Infants with early rickets are restless and sleep poorly; constant movement on the pillow denudes the head of occipital hair and suffer malnutrition. Such infants do not sit, crawl, or walk early, and the closing of the fontanels is delayed. Craniotabes (probably the earliest physical sign) is followed by enlargement of the epiphyseal cartilages of the long bones, particularly noticeable at the costochrondal junctions (rachitic rosary) and at the lower ends of the radius, ulna, tibia, and fibula. Weight-bearing bends the bones and causes deformities such as bowlegs, knock knees, and pigeon breast.

X-ray change precede clinical sign, becoming evident in the **third or fourth month** of life – **even at birth if the mother is deficient in vitamin D.Bone changes** are most evident at the lower ends of the radius and ulna. The diaphysial ends lose their sharp, clear outline, are cup shaped, and show a spotty or fringy rarefaction. Later, the distance between the ends of the radius and ulna and the metacarpal bones appears increased since the true ends are noncalcified and invisible. The shadows cast by the shaft decrease in density and the network formed by laminas becomes coarse. Characteristic deformities are produced by bending of the bones at the cartilage-shaft junction and in the substance of the shaft. As healing begins, a thin white line of calcification appears at the epiphysis, becoming denser and thicker as **calcification procedes.** Later, **lime salts** are deposited beneath the periosteum, the shaft casts a denser shadow, and the lamella disappear.

In, **adult deficiency** demineralization (osteomalacia) occurs, particularly in the spine, pelvis, and lower extremities; the fibrous lamellas become visible by x-ray and incomplete fissure-like fractures appear in the cortex.

As the **bones soften,** weight causes **bowing** of the **long bones,** vertical **shortening of the vertebrae** and flattening of the pelvic bones, which **alters the pelvic outlet.**

Rachitic tetany is caused by hypocalcemia, and may be accompanied by either infantile or adult vitamin D deficiency. The clinical findings are discussed under TETANY in Sec14 Ch7 and HYPOPARATHY.

In rickets and osteomalacia, serum calcium is maintained by the parathyroids, but serum phosphorous is low as a result of **diminished tubular resorption** (see TABLE 91 in Sec 24. Ch 6 for normal serum values). Alkaline phosphatise is increased. If the concentration of calcium (in mg/100 ml of serum) is multiplied by that of phosphorous, a value obtained which in the normal child is > 40. When it is < 30, rickets or osteomalacia is usually present.

A history of deficient vitamin D intake strongly suggests rickets and helps to distinguish it from infantile scurvy (see under VITAMIN C deficiency, below) and other conditions. **Congenital syphilis**; chrondodystrophy by the large head, short extremities, and thick bones, and by normal calcium, phosphorous, and phosphatise blood values. Other conditions such as osteogenisis imperfect, **cretinism, congenital dislocation of the hips,** hydrocephalus, and poliomyelitis should be readily distinguishable. Manifestation of tetany in infantile rickets must be differentiated from convulsions due to other causes. Cases of rickets not due to deficiency of vitamin D and include renal rickets, familial hypophosphatemic rickets, renal tubular acidosis, and Fanconi syndrome.

Osteomalacia must be differentiated from other causes of widespread bone decalcification (e.g., hyperanthyroidism, basophilic adenoma of the pituitary, andrenocortical tumor, multiple myeloma, and atrophy of disuse). Other signs of these diseases, **serum calcium/ phosphorous** and alkaline phosphatise **determinations,** and **x-ray findings determine the diagnosis.**

CHAPTER VII

Treatment of Vitamin D Deficiency

With adequate calcium/phosphorous intake, **adult osteomalacia** and **uncomplicated rickets** can be cured, slowly, by daily intake of vitamin D **400 U.S.P u.** Larger doses (**about 1600u, or more/day**) are more rapidly effective. The first evidence of improvement (a **rise in serum phosphorous**) occurs in about **10 days** followed in the **third week** by **x-ray signs of calcium and phosphorous deposition in the osseous tissues.** After about 1 month, the dosage can be reduced gradually to ordinary levels. If tetany is a complication, this treatment should be supplemented during the first week by calcium I.V. (see HYPOCALCEMIA AND TETANY in Sec 14, Ch. 7).

For refractory rickets, the dosage of vitamin D should be **increased** by 10,000 U.S.P u. Increments at 3-wk intervals until benefit is evident. As most patients respond to **50,000 or 60,000 u./day**, this may be the **starting dose.** Some patients require **1,000,000 to 1,500,000 u./day to induce healing, and from 150,000 to 300,000 u./day for maintenance.**

When larger doses (**20,000 U.S.P. u./day in infants and premature, 50,000 u./day in children**) are given in **rickets**, especially with co-existing renal insufficiency, the physician should be at guard for evidence of hypervitaminosis (q.v. in Sec 14, Ch. 3). Toxic manifestations may appear after the first sign of healing. The physician should make weekly or fortnightly examinations; if the dose is extremely large (100,000 U.S.P. u./day), at weekly or semiweekly intervals. If the dosage is not immediately lowered, as is ordinarily advisable, semiweekly serum calcium/phosphorous determinations should be made and the urine checked for calcium casts (these will not occur in acid urine). If the serum calcium level is .12mg/100ml, or if casts appear, treatment consists of stopping vitamin D immediately and keeping the uric acid.

When it is important to **cure rickets rapidly** (e.g., when weakness of the thorax menaces life), 50,000 U.S.P. u./day of vitamin D should be given, reduced to 1,200 u./day as soon as healing is evidenced by a rise in serum phosphorus or by x-ray. In the steatorreas, cod liver oil is contraindicated but vitamin D may be given in doses of 30,000 to 50,000 u. as concentrated fish oils, viosternol in oil or in propylene glycol, cholecalciferal, or oral or parenteral crystalline vitamine D.

FROM MARTINDALE (2):

RICKETS. The number of units required for the prevention of rickets lies between 500 and 1,500 daily, the daily requirement varying with age, rate of growth, presence or absence of infection, and the diet of the child. During the first few years 1000 to 1,500 units should be given daily, and this should be continued right through the summer. – C. Asher, Practitioner, 1940, 145, 61.

Although a daily intake of 500 units would probably protect most full term infants and young children from rickets, a daily allowance of 700 units would give a wider margin of safety. The premature infant (under 5 ½ lb.) required twice as much vitamin D as the full-term infant. Pregnant and nursing mothers should receive a supplement of 700 units daily.- Report of the Subcommittee of the British Paediatric Association, per Lancet, ii/1942, 460.

Bibliography (Section 1)

(1) The Merck Manual, 12 Edition, Merck & Co. Inc, 1972 (pp 1043-1046) REDACTED
(2) The Extra Pharmacopia, Martindale, Vol 1, 24th Edition, London, The Pharmaceutical Press, 1958 (pp 319-323) REDACTED

SECTION 2

CHAPTER VIII

Parenteral Vitamin D

Though a patient may eat large meals, if the stomach does not assimilate what is given, he is quite as poorly nourished as one who gets a crust a day. I am reminded of the line in one of the plays written by Shakespeare they are as sick that surfeit as they that starve with nothing. (1)

Wiki Overview has case studies on Vitamin D injections working on over 20 diseases. If this book or Wiki can't convince you – **NOBODY CAN. PLUS YOUR DOCTOR HAS TO ACTUALLY INJECT VITAMIN D. WITHOUT THIS – THIS BOOK IS USELESS.**

July 2, 2018

When Scanty Panty asked me to write down all my experiments and experiences with ultra violet light, I was thrilled. She was the motivating factor for me to fix my body in the first place. On the verge of collapse - I have never been able to relate to the outside world. In one movie they called them – giving up on life pants – and a friend said – he thought I was a person who was just hanging on. Just hanging on and it still hurts that he could see it. I needed more life and a better quality of life to justify my living.

All the web pages give good solutions. And I have tried many of them. **Scanty's main source of her oil was an ultra violet light. 275 watts of power and a cage that came with it. She poured 3 liters of canola oil in a glass pitcher and beamed the light at close distance through the open top and left the light on for 4 days. She sent me a glass jar of the product and she had me bathe in about a tablespoon of oil once a day. "a quick pour" out of a glass.**

She experimented on me before with a 5-hour oil about a year ago and I bathed in this oil for 6 months and then a 2-day oil for six months.

In her letter of directions Scanty wrote about Neils Finsen and the research his institute did on smallpox and lupus. He started a University and they experimented extensively on many other constitutional cases including syphilis, leprosy, and malnutrition. She sent me a book followed by three more.

About half as much as the symptoms you are experiencing but in reverse. **Using the 2 day oil will trigger untwisting.**

Chronic infection, chronic pain, and chronic diseases. This book gives a reliable cure for surface (local or acute) and whole body (constitutional or chronic) infections with a lot of practical evidence. Instructionally and all the details about ultraviolet light using references from four vintage medical handbooks and dictionaries. Like in the below article which explains about exposing a drug to ultraviolet light – somehow vitamin D is formed – this irradiation process takes this "vitamin" and turns it into a "drug" by its intensity. Not a real vitamin but a kind of forced metabolism to create an **anabolic hormonal steroid infusion** into the oil – Vitamin D. A moving and storing of mass. Of mass particles smaller than any other particle at the time. With deep penetration. Maybe closer to being an amphetamine. An upper taken internally.

CHAPTER IX

My Story with Scanty Panty

Long before I met Scanty Panty, I was already convinced Hippocrates was a guise for good intentions for future doctors. The only concept my doctors followed was the words: I do not know.

So I looked at what Hippocrates had to say – again – and discovered not one of my doctors treated my digestive and headache problems with any seriousness. Focusing on my mental state, I was prescribed anti-psychotics for a final placebo to a physical problem. I also had chronic breathing problems and an extremely low energy level. All my life.

This placated me until I took my first pill, and my stomach was sent into a tizzy. My doctor told me I needed to take – more drugs.

I already had drunk a tanker full of booze, smoked about five thousand packs of smokes, about twenty kilos of marijuana and hashish, drank another tanker of coffee, done cocaine, acid, opiates and opioids, and had about a dozen near death blackouts. Each remedy I found later in my homeopathic manual.

I had already used Scanty's Guitar Oil for a couple of years and my hands started healing. It worked well but when I started to think about whole body infections I started bathing in her 2 day oil. A tablespoon in my bath just didn't do the job. At first I felt better and then worse. The infection just kept coming back and when I thought I was doing well I told my friends and family. Every single time – I was flat on my back – convulsing within forty minutes after telling them. The cuts on my hands also closed up and opened up. Over and over again. Using a local remedy for a constitutional chronic infection just was not working.

I needed to take care of this whole body problems. Entirely.

The word pepsis stuck out. I had read that word before. I got it confused with sepsis. And it included the functions of the mouth to the "gut" the gastrointestinal tract.

I also read in this book that a person named Dr. Bob had had this same stomach problems which he proceeded to bombard with booze and drugs. More booze, drugs, and problems that you could possibly imagine – until I realized – I was just like him.

So I started bathing in Scanty's Finesse Oil – the 4 day oil. It's the trigger and the back-up plan.

I shower after every bath and use just over or under a tablespoon in the start of the bath. **I started dreaming immediately and my fingernails got harder.** Not bad for a guy who was incapacitated for a half a century. But it does not seem to be hitting my blood stream. I lacked oxygen. My body is still cold and I wonder if it is removing the calcium built right to my bones.

Is my body strong enough to take care of itself??

And – Can I take this oil orally like an anabolic steroid after all the calcium metabolism is complete?? Isn't it like taking the pharmaceuticals mentioned below but without the added calcium or yeast?? I mean to avoid the doctor because of the side effects mentioned below and make a cheap and constant source of Vitamin D?? And quite frankly, I was afraid of the symptoms coming back by just bathing in the oil. And more candidly, there was a pain in my groin like a twist so deep that all the bathing was not doing the job. Not 100%. Why not start taking this now?? Orally. I made the 2 day oil and sat there looking at it.

I rechecked the other sources about over calcification using pharmaceutical information about calciferol and ergosternol and started to wonder if the use of a calcium or yeast base was well intentioned or just another way to – get a patent – plus the symptoms of over or long term usage was in fact something other than Vitamin D so a doctor was definitely needed. I could however see the logic in their way of medicine. Like inoculation. And Hippocrates.

So I became curious. I knew that years after Finsen's death they discovered that ultra violet radiation created Vitamin D and they started using it to fortify milk and possibly animal feed (and indoor chickens). In a 1970's Merck Manual they said they recently discovered the flow of calcium being freed in the mucous membranes. Now they have been irradiating yeast and what could have been the white part of oyster shells, in drugs, since the 30's. But in the British Martindale's manual (from 1958) they knew Vitamin D deficiency was the cause of many metabolism problems. In fact they traced this metabolism problem caused by Vitamin D deficiency to scurvy (Vitamin C deficiency) and skin problems (Vitamin E deficiency) anemia (iron deficiency), and a complete breakdown of calcium and phosphorous metabolism creating improper bone formation and nutritional absorption. So I wondered about Vitamin A & B deficiencies and the medical problems they cause and – what is the chemical composition of a cancer node. Assimilation.

So I went to the internet about the composition of a cancer node and I found nothing. Elimination. Pepsis.

It's like Hippocrates, my doctor and every doctor since – the internet just didn't know.

So I took it further. If they don't know the chemical composition of a cancer node – one was taken out of my forehead and analyzed – and a "spot" or "shadow" or "scarring " appeared around or in my right lung years ago (they just knew what it wasn't) – then what is it are they trying to cure?? And why was it that all the research done by the about twenty different institutes was – forgotten – remembered – and forgotten again. Mal = Evil. I made the 2 day oil.

I experimented with orally consuming the 4 day oil about a month and a half ago when Scanty was still out of town. My rationale was that babies were being administered olive oil orally as a laxative and simply thought it couldn't hurt. 1 drop would clear my sinuses, 2 my throat, 3 my chest and 4 my stomach. 10 my kidneys.

The effect of the drug is instant. The speed of light. It moves in mass mucous. I simply poured 1-10 drops into my **hot** beverage – 3 times a day for 1.5 months.

CHAPTER X

CALCIFEROL and other FAT-SOLUBLE VITAMINS

Vitamin D. Under this term are included several substances possessing the property of **preventing** or **curing rickets.** These substances are derivatives of sterols which acquire **antirachitic** properties when exposed to **ultra-violet light.** The two most important properties are **calciferol** and activated 7-dehydrocholesterol which are produced respectively by thc **irradiation** of ergosterol and of 7-dehydrocholesterol.

Calciferol (B.P., I.P.). Vitamin D2: Ergocalciferol; **Irradiated** Ergosterol; **Viosterol.** 24-methyl-9:10-secocholesta-7: 10(19):22-tetraen-3-ol. C28H44O=396.7.

Dose:

Prophylactic, for **infants** and **adults,** 0.025 to .1 mg. (1/2400 to 1/600 grain; **1000 to 4000 units) daily.** Foreign Pharmacopoeias: In Belg., Chil., Chin., Cz., Dan., Egyp., Fr., Hung., Ind., Jug., Pol., Swed., Swiss, U.S.

An **antirachitic** substance obtained from **ergosterol,** a sterol occurring in **yeast,** by **ultra-violet irradiation.** Colorless, odorless, tasteless, acicular crystals. It contains **40,000 units** of **antirachitic** activity (vitamin D) in **1 mg.**

Insoluble in water; soluble in alcohol, ether, chloroform, and acetone; soluble in 1 in 50 to 100 of fixed oils. It should be stored in sealed **glass containers,** from which the air has been evacuated, or replaced by inert gas, protected from light, in a cool place.

Toxic effects. The toxic dose of **calciferol is many times the therapeutic dose,** and single doses of **1,000,000 units** or more have been given **without untoward effects. Prolonged administration** of doses of **100,000 to 150,000** units daily is liable to give rise to **toxic symptoms** in about 20% of patients. The **symptoms** of overdosage are loss of appetite, lassitude, pallor, polyuria, profuse sweating, extreme thirst, constipation, or diarrhoea, vomiting, headache and loss of weight. These call for discontinuance of the drug, and **resumption in a smaller dose** when the symptoms subside. If intolerance persists treatment must be abandoned, as continued overdosage may cause **abnormal deposition of calcium** in various parts of the body which may lead to formation of renal **calculi**, osteoporosis, arterioschlerosis, and even death. It is advisable to make monthly estimations of the serum calcium during treatment, and if the level rises persistently above 12 mg. per 100 ml. the drug should be discontinued, even in the absence of toxic symptoms, until the calcium has fallen to a normal level (9 to 11 mg. per 100 ml.). (2)

CHAPTER XI

The Absence of Scanty Panty

Scanty Panty had been out of town for a month and a half and that fomented the trouble. I had been bathing in her 4-day oil as per her instructions – but consumed 1-10 drops – 3 times a day orally. And she had returned with my 275 watt light package and got me going on my first batch of 2 day oil before she left. Bathing bathing and bathing. This was all that I had been doing since she had sent me my last package of three litres of 4-day oil and my body is feeling great. But 1.5 months and something had been missing or something had still been there. It gave me a feeling of imminent doom and a really bad stomach ache. That propelled to hit myself in both sides of my head.

My body did feel good. There was an improvement. My fingers healed by over eighty five percent. However, my muscles were sore. My convulsions were periodically uncramping. But there was something amiss. I still felt woozy and was on the verge of collapse. Though this was intermittent, the period of normalcy was no way redeeming.

When we were setting up the light I could feel it. She was backtracking her experiments. 2 days of pure uv light treatment in three litres of canola. I couldn't just stop looking at the bright yellow light the canola oil was making under that intense light source. I tried to refrain from touching the jar but temptation took the better of me.

I knew it before she left because I read the above dosages of Vitamin D in the cure of infantile rickets and adult osteomalacia. This was not only in the methods of usage but also in the dosages and durations. I knew I was going to really start experimenting with this oil. But I needed to put a time frame on the process similar to the below. 2 months – 4 day oil and 2 weeks off. 2 months – 2 day oil and 2 weeks off. Repeat 2 day oil. 12 months for adequate treatment. So now I am up to 1 teaspoon 3 times a day of the 2 day oil.

So here is what that manual said that put something into my head – "the first evidence of improvement (a rise in serum phosphorous) occurs in about **10 days**, followed in the **third week by x-ray signs** of calcium and phosphorous deposition in the osseous tissues. After about **1 mo.**, the dosage can be **reduced gradually** to ordinary levels." (5)

And very interesting a couple of pages before – "after adequate treatment, degeneration of the cartilage cells within 24 hr and the penetration by a vascular network within 48 hr permit calcium and phosphorous deposition. Osteoid material at the diaphysis ceases to form and normal endochrondal **production of new bone resumes**. In adults, **osteoid** signs of deficiency are similarily **reversed**: the **cancellous bone** of the diaphysis **dissappears** and the cortical **bone is resorbed**." (5)

One of the ancient quotes possibly attributed to Hippocrates said all problems with health start and end in the stomach. I read this after I started this treatment. I don't think this great man came up with this idea – it was the first idea that was passed on to him either through his first hand experiences or his own.

But if we enter a hypothetical world. A world where a new disease isn't invented every day. It's like that book starting with Hippocrates. Before him the world thought there was only one disease and the cure was water, air heat, sun, earth. Always the same and lots of it. Think – leper colony. Well maybe this bathing process takes all the bad and "dead cells" out of our bodies and makes our body ready to cure anything. And everything including "dead cells" because they can be reactivated if not moved (you can't destroy energy)

This book was meant to be for addicts and junkies. The infirm and the incarcerated. **Definitely wipe on the same amount of oil – three fingertips wiped on hands first then three fingertips on arms, legs and chest.** And drink it – as much as you can handle. Metabolize calcium deposits from your skin to your bones and move phosphorous from all your organs by wiping and drinking it. But one thing happened in the meantime. I believed allopathy as well as homeopathy are "make work" schemes. I went broke and could not afford even the simplest of medications. This happens to people of all walks of life. Did I mention my light cost me five dollars plus tax at a junk store?

So anyways. So anyways. So anyways. The details. The details. The details.

CHAPTER XII

Affordable Healthcare- Not a Dream

Affording health care. That's wishful thinking – what if you cannot afford the drugs ...

Ultraviolet. Noting the actinic or chemical rays beyond the violet end of the spectrum; **extra-vital u.** includes rays of the wavelengths of 2,900 to I.850 A.u. **intravital u.**, having wavelengths between 3,900 and 3,200 A.u. **vital u.**, rays necessary or helpful to **normal growth**, promoting **calcium metabolism**, and **antirachitic** in action, having the wavelengths between 3,200 and 2,900 A.u.

Rickets [E. ***wrick*, to twist.**] Rachitis, a disease, occurring in infants and young children; it is characterized by softening of the bones, enlargement of the liver and spleen, **malnutrition**, profuse sweating, and general tenderness of the body when touched. **Acute r.** infantile scurvy. **Adult r.**, a disease resembling rickets in many of its features, occurring in adult life.

Rickety. Rachitic, suffering from rickets.

Viosterol (vi-os'ter-ol). Ergosterol subjected to ultraviolet radiation by which an antirachitic (vitamin D)potency is developed. V. in oil, v. dissolved in a vegetable oil and standardized to a definite potency. (3)

Now the **white irradiation light** is assumed to have the entire spectrum of ultraviolet spectrum some of it assumed to be very destructive to living organisms in modern literature. So I was very careful of the possibility of overdoing the hours of **canola oil** exposure, the number of drops in the bath, as well as the number of baths in a week. I let my body decide.

• • •

Now I am keeping the amount of quotes to a minimum to avoid too much information as well as respect copyright law. People with access to doctors will have access to information much more detailed but details for specific diseases **(Caries (cavities), Chilblains (heat rash), Chromoblastomycosis, Ciliac Disease, Exema, Leprosy, Lupus Vulgaris, Pulmonary Tuberculosis, Rickets, and Tuberculosis Glands)** are given in the **Martindale Pharmacopia** citing test results from the **twenty different institutes** including success rates and **dosages**. But what both processes seem to do is to eliminate all other drugs and replace them with one drug – a highly concentrated vitamin D. The information should include the hazards of long term health problems of vitamin D deficiency and that in most cases all problems can be **reversed**. Making the drug at home is not only inventive but the bathing process allows the drug to enter through our skin – the same way it absorbs it from nature. Bath – local = acute. Ingest – chronic = constitutional = metabolism. Mucous system = immunity system.

So why go back to pre Hippocrates methods of cure. Well nature is the basis of all modern medicine with its abundant contents of minerals and plants. It also contains air, water, and fire. So as far as danger goes, consuming large amounts of any plant or mineral will kill us – including vitamin D. And like sunshine - too much is too much. But the process of how nature cured itself before man took over is an interesting concept. And bathing and sunshine were the cures that animals and plants used – without any help from humans.

And like I say – people like to invent things – and then call it their own. Remember for less than fifty dollars you can cure yourself – and through the experience of one man, I can vouch that a simple bathing process is all you need for local infections. Now for constitutional chronic problems – a problem that remains for more than 3 or 6 months or occurs every year or so - I think this might be indicative enough to get things started. But words have a problem describing simple things. Like the feeling of poverty and being left behind or treated unfairly or physically not able to meet the demands of life – or like with childhood chronic pain – being alone, scared, and afraid.

So here is what was decided for me to do ... and I have to say now I was driven to do this like my body craved the action of ingesting the 2 day oil.

I dropped a teaspoon of it in my hot coffee.

And by this time the mucous was literally washing down from the top of my nasal passages through my neck and the top of my chest – mixing with the lower mucous membranes. This flowing or mucous membranes is the most invigorating thing I have ever felt.

CHAPTER XIII

Solar- The Indispensable Warrior

Sunlight is the easiest energy that can be harnessed. By Scanty Panty's method I simply shined a white ultraviolet bulb of 275-watt intensity into three liters of canola for 2 and 4 days and created a power that is enough to cure one person. By my calculations that would mean 3 and 6 days using the 175 watt light bulb I saw at the hardware store.

If my knowledge serves me right, two Nobel Prizes were awarded to two different people in two different years in the early nineteen hundreds (Niels Finsen) for their experiments with UV and later x-ray technology and radiation treatment were used to cure infectious diseases. Finsen had low energy.

Not a bad idea for the patient but for the technician – overexposure meant certain fates unimaginable for mice and men at that time.

So I was very careful to follow Scanty's instructions. I am still not used to it and actually utilize it as a heat lamp instead of a heater. But I am the first one to admit I can never get truly used to the blandness of the frequency of the light.

It may appear a little simplistic to say but, just perhaps, maybe, just what if?? Chronic pain and chronic diseases are caused by:

Pain is always an indication of inflammation or congestion; it is a cry for relief, the danger signal, and a nurse should never disregard its warning. Inflammation usually has several unmistakable symptoms, such as heat, redness, swelling or pain which may be the result of **internal congestion**, an injury to the tissues caused by fracture, a burn, an abscess, or a boil.

This book was meant to include stories and the names and lives of people whose lives were cut short by a mysterious and sudden death. Chris Cornell was the latest one to occur by his own hands and Prince – someone from my hometown and possibly at the age I am now.

I mention these two now because it was very unusual of me to break down after hearing the news. Another thing that I said out loud after both their deaths was – they died of what I have.

Growing up in a rock and roll world – whether as a listener or a critic, a player or a watcher – I mean I have done all four – I couldn't help but wonder "why so suddenly" and every time any of my friends has died, it has been sudden. At the funerals I always heard about the mysteriousness from the parents and other friends.

I bring this up because I have posted the obituaries of the older guys like Lux Interior and Jim Carroll on my bathroom wall. A place where they would want them to be. But for Prince and Mr. Cornell I did not celebrate their wonderful lives. All I did was shrink into my basement – ball my head off – and think – they had what I have.

But the last quote may explain all the sudden and mysterious deaths of my friends. I hope to settle confusion for those with friends like my dead friends.

CHAPTER XIV

Terminating the Terminal

December 18, 2018

Now I am trying to keep this in the present tense and since I have never consciously experienced a normal body I am having a hard time writing about what normal really is.

So I understand the convulsions and how certain very successful treatments involve inducing the exact symptom the disease is causing. But this deep rooted ripping and twisting – this slow reversal of some final reversal of the final slow – untwist – I cannot predict – but they happen quite slowly I can regain my composure in between.

It does hurt but I smile in between knowing this pain level is way less than half as bad as before.

December 20, 2018

A change in attitude. I mean this is the real change we are looking for.

So I grabbed the 4 day oil and I did exactly what I did at the beginning.

December 21, 2018

I mean it's hard to grasp the last movement on video. But after the last one all I did was go upstairs to grab a cup of coffee. I was going to do a squat but I lowered myself just four inches and twisted and that was enough. I came downstairs and felt another twist and that was it. Nothing alarming. No weird stuff going on. No big pain.

I still have until January 2 to the 6 month period of treatment – and 500 words – so I am feeling fairly optimistic – at least for now. I just dropped 10 drops off a screwdriver into my second coffee so that twenty drops and it's not ever 7:30 AM – and that with the 4 day oil.

So that was – 2 months bathing in a tablespoon and consuming 1-10 drops 3 times daily of the 4 day oil – 2 months bathing in a tablespoon and consuming 1 teaspoon 3 times daily of the 2 day oil – and then back to the 1-10 drops with the 4 day oil alternating until 50 weeks. That one bath a day followed by a shower. **2 – 2 week periods not drinking product when my body felt like – TOO MUCH OIL.**

There is one interesting thing I would like to mention. Sometimes I wait until half my coffee is done before I put in my dosage of oil because it makes it more potent and you can feel the effect instantaneously. There are quite a few times when I like doing it.

March 22, 2019

It's just what I thought it was going to be. Double nickels on the dime. Pants grimy on the insides. Socks and underwear turned inside out just like the t-shirts. Real greasy living.

Remember and I am saying this to remind myself repeatedly. I need to go with the flow.

And always remember – ALL diseases are caused by a faulty constitution – and the effects of ALL diseases no matter how scary the name – can always be – **REVERSED.**

May 22, 2019

There is a loss of breath & then a body movement.
All my breath is in a wheeze
Am I dying?

9:27 AM Feb 11, 2013

I just thought I would start out by recalling the major symptoms. I was feeling the same 6 years ago. and say everything was the same until just a few minutes ago. It seems however to me that with this treatment it has been 1 – a body movement and 2 – loss of breath.

So why end with the symptoms we are trying to get rid of?? Well just to show that no matter what we thought – the malady originated in the stomach and not the lungs or the limbs.

The amazing thing is that there are no bad emissions no bad taste and weird colored bile. It is totally devoid of anything peculiar.

I just tried a lot of guessing and analyzing before and after a shower as to in which muscle or joint the pain originated in. All the earthy matter was removed from the stomach – digestion was perfect – metabolism flawless – and hopefully an impeccable immune system.

July 4, 2021

If I were to tell you the last twist of my body was with my fingers in between my heart and lungs right by the valve and where a shadow showed up on an x-ray – would you think that that can happen to you??

CHAPTER XV

My Experiments with Pain

It was to test if my body would be able to move the remaining mucous and calcification. I grew my nails for ten weeks to test their hardness. Now, my fingers feel dexterous and fully healed.

I FEEL NO PAIN. THERE IS NO INFLAMMATION IN MY BODY.

MY LUNGS WORK AT FULL CAPACITY AND MY CIRCULATION IS PERFECT.

The 4 day oil is SCANTY PANTY GUITAR OIL.

The 2 day oil ENERGIZED MY PRIVATES.

So knowing this energy transference this Newtonian moving of mass could happen I read about how to create Vitamin D using a UV light which I bought at a thrift shop. A tanning **SUNLAMP** which **LIZARD LIGHT** will direct you to **EXOTERRA.COM FOLLOWED LIGHTING AND CONSEQUENTLY SOLAR GLOW**. I think that the heat intensity of my bulb at 275 Watts is really HOT. This one may be better. But do remember the **LIGHT CAGE TOO.**

This Vitamin D making was discovered in the 1930's and chemical changes can be made by using high frequency light contained in certain wavelengths by isolating those rays – found in THE SUN.

My tests 60 months prior had me using only one method of Vitamin D which is now contained in my Scanty Panty's Panacea Cure. It was working in curing severe chronic inflammation – using **reversal of pain** as a guide.

I had 2 months of drinking 5-10 drops and also bathing in a quick pour of the 4-day oil for 2 months

Later, I had 2 months of drinking about 15 drops 3 times a day and then bathing in a quick pour of the 2-day oil

As described in book this rotated for **1 Year** then.

I STOPPED INGESTION OF OIL AND USING IT IN BATH. BUT I BATHED AND SHOWERED ALMOST EVERYDAY.

ABOUT 60 MONTHS I WILL GAIN PERFECT FOOD DIGESTION AND METABOLISM CREATING HARD HEALTHY BONES, TEETH FINGERNAILS AND PERFECT BLOOD AND LYMPHATIC CIRCULATION.

I HAD ZERO LETHARGY AND FATIGUE. I HAD PERFECT PROCREATION ABILITIES AND A HEALTHY SEXUAL APPETITE. MY THOUGHTS WERE ALSO ARTICULATE.

CHAPTER XVI

Reflections

September 27, 2021

I am gazing at a guitar and watching a movie. I am going to light an old coffee perculator of 3 litres of canola oil for 100 hrs. using a 275 UV light. This will make Vitamin D in a potency to make a drug like commercially bought drugs like calciferol without calcium. I am wondering if I could **use water instead of oil** - bottle God and cure World Disease.

There's a new webpage on Wikipedia that I found on Vitamin D about how to cure coronavirus and 20 other diseases and another on the NCBI website called **Vitamin D and the anti-viral state.** This isn't an alternative cure. There are a plethora of case studies using Vitamin D cited in my books and an another thousand on the internet. Wikipedia has many on COV-19 alone.

What's very distressing is that there is another epidemic on the verge of breaking out. The entire day I am trying to finish off this book and I am reading about cold viruses and bacteria. Gout. The frustrating part is that it interferes with prevention of **all problems solved holistically.** The quest for the perfect metabolism persists. I am on the lookout for a perfect metabolism to solve existing problems as well as to conquer future potential maladies.

What we need is a brand new body. For all ages.

Climate change is another matter of concern. How do we **adapt** ourselves to this impending disaster?? A healthy body should be able to withstand any weather. We need a perfect body that will acclimatise to the evolving day to day weather.

A cheap solution for the common man. Order the light and make your solution or arrange an appointment with your doctor. We will mix the first two books.

First let the fingers do the walking. It's an external skin test. Watch your wounds on your hands show you there is something working. Harder fingernails?? Use as hand oil on all parts of body and see what happens. Use to regenerate wood dipping a square of old flannel as a reusable cloth. Get more comfortable with oil. Use the 4 day oil – 2 months and then the 2 day oil – 2 months.

That is how I tested the process and the healing gave me confidence – a drive to **bathe** in the oil took over. I wanted more. I beamed the canola to 4 day oil to create an effect – a change – and then bathed in a splash of the oil and **thendrank** 15-30-45 drops a day for two months. Repeat for two months with 2 day oil.

Look at the results. See how my confidence level has automatically increased.

My symptoms decreased. But that **change in my dream pattern** happened in days after starting and my **fingernails got stronger.**

Doctors have been using Vitamin D with or without calcium now. But to avoid over-calcification the injection has minimized this hazard. **This book gives more information from studies including doses.** Doctors injecting Vitamin D? Why not!

Better longevity and curing world hunger is not an experiment. It's been reality for over 100 years. Here is where we started 30 years after Niels Finsen invented an Ultra Violet light bulb and accidentally made Vitamin D. It's what we all want.

He saw results a year after using direct light I used a different process. After a year or so of experiment there was a change. Neither Niels nor I am above average intelligence.

This is the process to start on a perfect constitution. With a perfect constitution we have perfect metabolism and simultaneously a perfect immune system. **If you are a doctor your information starts later for dosages** and many past tests on this drug.

For a poor constitution this is for a year and then keep bathing and not drinking the oil. 12 months later you will have a perfect constitution.

CHAPTER XVII

In Conclusion

October 27, 2021

So this book is for doctors and YOU. So far, I have sent out 300,000 emails to the media, cops, judges, PMs MPs at a strike rate of 7,000 per month.

A billion emails later I found out 99 percent of my nasty email readers had imperfect constitutions – TOO FAT, TOO SKINNY, TOO SMART, TOO STUPID, LOW SELF ESTEEM. IN FACT WITHIN DAYS I FOUND OUT - PEOPLE WERE LIKE ME.

NOT EVERYBODY HAS FEAR.

And what we wanted was sexy bodies with a perfect skin and the result of a perfect healing system – longevity and the most comfortable life. And more money of course more money. But above all – we wanted perfection.

HEALTH. MORE LIFE.

The most important thing in the world was my dad telling my brother – this is not your life – and between the two of them they have 8 university degrees while I only one. I was the quintensential underachiever good for nothing from the outside and from the inside. I felt my life was dispensable until a few days ago really.

The way you save the world from bad health is in these books. There is enough information for your doctor or you to get started. One advantage of the home remedy is you can personally feel the reversal of your symptoms. It's interesting in the least for the curious. The doctor can run tests for blood to make sure there is a positive change and x-rays too.

Both will require this:
Bone Reformation.

November 3, 2021

If you had checked your body when you were 21 and every decade after that and you find your body deteriorating – **it's not normal.**

December 2, 2021

Bone growth feels like growing pain reversal. It hurts.

What we are doing here is stripping all foreign matter from our bodies to the bone so that the bone can grow again. Revitalising our organs and transportation system of nerves and veins is essential so that our bodies can – regrow – healthy.

Now we can do this at any age. Reverse the process of growing old with – new growth.

This foreign matter originates from nature. It's the air and the land and the little particles of energy accumulated in our bodies. There is this calcium component that evolves from thin and clear to thick white and hard with time. When this coats the bone organs and transportation systems in ANY LIVING THING aging or degeneration occurs.

It sounds so painless to reverse this process but it there is 50% of the pain that I felt in the past. Vitamin D loosens the mineral portion setting it free of its contents to its disposal system through all our organs. Making it is easy –

Beam canola oil for 2 days and 4 days using a 275-watt UV light from EXO TERRA used for keeping lizards and plants alive – 3 litres or better yet 3 quarts of each. Use a steel or glass container so that the atoms of light – photons - get trapped in the oil and after a day the radiation gets lesser and it can be consumed internally.

Here is what I did to reverse the age processing. I drank 1-3 teaspoons 3 times a day of the 4-day oil while bathing in the same oil for 2 months. About 2 tablespoons is – a quick pour out of any glass cup. The potent oil will activate a drug reaction – an effect where the convulsions start.

They loosen up the white build up in the stomach, liver, kidneys and heart when you drink it. I did this for two months of the 4-day oil followed by two months of the 2-day oil. Then I stopped drinking the oil while bathing in the 2 day oil.

I did the above again. After a year, I stopped both the oils but bathed every day. The body takes over from here – the body and the heat from the bath.

The light photons are smaller than electricity particles and every atom of solid matter on the planet. Its radiation from the sun in this case makes the transition in energy.

Metabolizing and after a year my own system slowly took over. As more matter was used or removed – my metabolism got stronger – constitution got stronger – and immunity system – almost bulletproof.

September 18, 2023

When I started trying to save my own life I had to ask myself – DO YOU WANT TO LIVE?? And the answer was a NO. The point of the experiment was to give evidence that even if someone feeling as dismal as me – could save his own life – even if he really cared two hoots.

But I wondered. Now I am 60 and if I counted back I would be 20 when my father was 60. What if I put myself at age 20? At first, I shuddered like my last body movement and then I thought – interesting.

If I did that with my now bulletproof like body – **MY LIFE IS GOING TO BE JUST FANTASTIC.**

This is from **Martindale (5):**

LUPUS VULGARIS. With the Finsen treatment a **recovery rate of 80%** has been achieved **in lupus** patients. Of the **remaining 20%** (130 cases) more than 60% have become **symptom free** with calciferol. The routine followed at the Finsen Institute is to give 180,000 units in an alcoholic solution daily for a month, reduced to 120,000 to 150,000 units as long as the patient remains in hospital, and then 90,000 units daily. Every patient receives 1.5 pints of milk daily. – S. Lomholt, Brit. J. J. Derm., 1948, 60, 132

Intramuscular injections of 600,000 units twice weekly, or 150,000 units daily **by mouth** in 28 cases. In 20 cases of lupus improvement was observed in 3 to 6 weeks, often preceded by a **flare-up** of the condition. In some cases the addition of local therapy hastened the progress. Fourteen patients were discharged free from active lupus. In 2 cases of obstinate, cervical adenitis results were pleasing, after an acute **preliminary flare-up.** Toxicity, usually mild, were present in 50% of cases. – D.E. Macrae, Lancet, i/1947, 135.

Since **lupus vulgaris** is a **relatively harmless** disease amenable to simple lines of treatment, calciferol in **massive doses** should only be uses in selective cases under **strict supervision.** – J.T. Ingram et al., Brit. J. Derm., 1948, 60, 159.

A daily dose of 4-5 mg. (180,000 units) of calciferol was given for 3 weeks to 284 patients with **lupus vulgaris** at the **Finsen Institute,** Copenhagen; thereafter this was adjusted to individual tolerance. Treatment was continued until there was **clinical and pathological evidence of cure for at least a year,** or until a total dose of not less than 1 g. of calciferol has been given; most patients required 600 to 600 mg. The patient were kept **under observation for an average of 5 years.** Of 271 patients who completed the course **(78.5%) became symptom - free.** At the end of the observation period, 120 (42.25%) had relapsed , 83 (29.25%) remained free of disease, and 20 (7%) were lost to follow-up. Treatment of relapsed patients were **increasingly less effective.** After a second course 45.5% of patients became symptom-free, and after a third course only 30.4%. The relapse rate was high, and an increasing number of patients showed signs of intolerance. Calciferol was contraindicated in the cases of erythema induratum and in pulmonary tuberculosis. – P.V. Marcussen, Dan med. Bull., 1955, 2, 129.

Calciferol by intramuscular injection is a better mode of treatment than calciferol in tablet form for the following reasons: (1) results are more rapid; (2) pigmentation is absent; (3) there are no toxic symptoms; (4) there is little or no hypercalcemia; (5) all patients do not get a packed red-cell volume; (6) the blood urea is raised in a smaller proportion of cases. Injections of 600,000 units were given 3 times weekly for the first 3 weeks and then twice weekly. Kidney function was impaired in all patients treated with calciferol for a considerable time; whether by injection or by mouth, and **treatment should not last longer than 4 months without a rest period.** – T. Lightbound, Lancet, ii/1948, 1010.

Combined treatment (in 7 cases) with **calciferol and streptomycin** was so effective as to suggest the 2 drugs are of benefit, usually **from 5 to 12 months.** Streptomycin, 1g. Daily intramusculatly in divided doses every 4 hours, was then used in combination with the calciferol until **the lesions appeared to be inactive;** this required from 6 to 9 weeks. A striking feature, besides the **rapid and uneventful healing of the lesions,** was the thin even atrophic character of the scars, which were relatively inconspicuous. – T. Cornbleet, J. Amer. Med. Ass., 1948, 138, 1150.

PULMONARY TUBERCULOSIS. Dosage varied from 500,000 to 3,000,000 units, and length of treatment was from 20-50 days. Initially 25,000 was given with 3 mg. of vitamin B1 daily, increasing to 100,000 units daily. Of 21 patients treated, none showed significant improvement in the lung condition. – P.J. Feeny, et al., Lancet, i/1947, 438. R.W. Carslaw, ibid., 616.

ECZEMA AND NEURODERMATITIS. Satisfactory clinical results were obtained in 15 cases of resistant or chronic relapsing excema and neurodermatitis by administration of large doses of vitamin D2. Cholesterol levels, usually found to be increased before treatment became normal during healing of the skin lesions. – W. Ludwig, Hautarzt, 1953, 4, 524, per Abstr. World Med., 1954, 15, 428.

In 88 cases of **eczema remarkably rapid regression condition of the acute inflammatory condition was obtained** with 6 intravenous injections of 15 mg. of vitamin D hydrosol (Vi-De-Hydrosol, preparation of calciferol in aqueous solution) at intervals of 1 to 2 or at the most 3 days. The hydrosol must be **injected very slowly** to avoid side effects characterized by flushing of the face, dyspnea, and **afeeling of constriction and anxiety.** - A. Schnitzer, Dermatologica, Basel, 1954, 108, 332.

TUBERCULOUS GLANDS. In 5 cases tuberculous glands were treated with calciferol 50,000 units daily. The observation suggested that **calciferol in high dosage may be beneficial in tuberculous conditions other than lupus vulgaris.** – H. J. Wallace, Lancet, ii/1946, 88.

Tuberculous manifestations of slow evolution – adentitis, tenosynovitis, lupus and diseases in the **small joints** – without fever and of hyperplastic type are most likely to respond favourably. The average daily dose (in tablets) for an adult is 100,000 units daily, though during the first few months of treatment the dosage should be larger. – G. B. Dowling, Brit. J. Derm., 1948, 60, 137.

Bibliography (Section 2)

(1) The Peoples Common Sense Medical Advisor, R.V. Pierce, MD, 98th Edition, World's Dispensary Medical Association, Copyright Canada 1914, revised 1926

(2) The Merck Manual, 12 Edition, Merck & Co. Inc, 1972 (pp 1043-1046) REDACTED

(3) Steadman's Medical Dictionary, Thomas Lathrop Steadman, A.M., M.D., 12th Revised Edition, Williams and Wilkins, England, 1933-34

(4) Taber's Cyclopedic Medical Dictionary, F. A. Davis Company, 17th Edition, USA, 1993 (p 1996)

(5) The Extra Pharmacopia, Martindale, Vol 1, 24th Edition, London, The Pharmaceutical Press, 1958 (pp 319-323) REDACTED

SECTION 3

CHAPTER XVIII

SAVING LIVES

There is a principal which is a bar against all information, which is proof against all arguments and which cannot fail to keep man in everlasting ignorance – That principle is contempt prior to investigation.
- Herbert Spencer

Though a patient may eat large meals, if the stomach does not assimilate what is given it, such a patient is quite as poorly nourished as one who gets a crust a day. (1)

Pain is always an indication of inflammation or congestion; it is a cry for relief, the danger signal, and a nurse should never disregard its warning. Inflammation usually has several unmistakable symptoms, such as heat, redness, swelling or pain which may be the result of internal congestion, an injury to the tissues caused by fracture, a burn, an abscess, or a boil, etc. (1)

Terminal infection, infection appearing in the late stage of another disease; often fatal. (2)

Ultraviolet. Noting the actinic or chemical rays beyond the violet end of the spectrum; **extra-vital u.** includes rays of the wavelengths of 2,900 to I.850 A.u. **intravital u.**, having wavelengths between 3,900 and 3,200 A.u. **vital u.**, rays necessary or helpful to **normal growth,**

promoting **calcium metabolism**, and **antirachitic** in action, having the **wavelengths** between 3,200 and 2,900 A.u.

Rickets [E. ***wrick*, to twist.**] Rachitis, a disease, occurring in **infants and young children; it is characterized by** softening of the bones, **enlargement of the liver and spleen, malnutrition, profuse sweating, and general tenderness of the body when touched.Acute r.** infantile scurvy. **Adult r.**, a disease resembling rickets in many of its features, occurring in **adult life.**

CALCIFEROL(5) and other FAT-SOLUBLE VITAMINS

Vitamin D. Under this term are included several substances possessing the property of **preventing** or **curing rickets.** These substances are derivatives of sterols which acquire **antirachitic** properties when exposed to **ultra-violet light.** The two most important are **calciferol** and activated 7-dehydrocholesterol which are produced respectively by the **irradiation** of ergosterol and of 7-dehydrocholesterol.

Calciferol (B.P., I.P.). Vitamin D2: Ergocalciferol; **Irradiated** Ergosterol; **Viosterol.** 24-methyl-9:10-secocholesta-7: 10(19):22-tetraen-3-ol. C28H44O=396.7.

*Dose:***Prophylactic,** for **infants** and **adults,** 0.025 to .1 mg. (1/2400 to 1/600 grain; **1000 to 4000 units) daily.**

Foreign Pharmacopoeias: In Belg., Chil., Chin., Cz., Dan., Egyp., Fr., Hung., Ind., Jug., Pol., Swed., Swiss, U.S.

An **antirachitic** substance obtained from **ergosterol**, a sterol occurring in **yeast**, by **ultra-violet irradiation**. Colorless, odorless, tasteless, acicular crystals. It contains **40,000 units** of **antirachitic** activity (vitamin D) in **1 mg**.

Insoluble in water; soluble in alcohol, ether, chloroform, and acetone; soluble in 1 in 50 to 100 of fixed oils. It should be stored in sealed **glass containers,** from which the air has been evacuated, or replaced by inert gas, protected from light, in a cool place.

Toxic effects. The toxic dose of **calciferol is many times the therapeutic dose,** and single doses of **1,000,000 units** or more have been given **without untoward effects. Prolonged administration** of doses of **100,000 to 150,000** units **daily** is liable to give rise to **toxic symptoms** in about 20% of patients. The **symptoms of overdosage** are loss of appetite, lassitude, pallor, polyuria, profuse sweating, extreme thirst, constipation, or diarrhoea, vomiting, headache and loss of weight. These call for discontinuance of the drug, and **resumption in a smaller dose** when the symptoms have subsided. If intolerance persists treatment must be abandoned, as continued overdosage may cause **abnormal deposition of calcium** in various parts of the body which may lead to formation of renal **calculi**, osteoporosis, arterioschlerosis, and even death. **It is advisable to make monthly estimations of the serum calcium during treatment**, and if the level rises persistently above 12 mg. per 100 ml. the drug should be discontinued, even in the absence of toxic symptoms, until the calcium has fallen to a normal level (9 to 11 mg. per 100 ml.). (1)

This is from **Martindale (5):**

LUPUS VULGARIS. With the Finsen treatment a **recovery rate of 80%** has been achieved **in lupus** patients. Of the **remaining 20%** (130 cases) more than 60% have become **symptom free** with calciferol. The routine followed at the Finsen Institute is to give 180,000 units in an alcoholic solution daily for a month, reduced to 120,000 to 150,000 units as long as the patient remains in hospital, and then 90,000 units daily. Every patient receives 1.5 pints of milk daily. – S. Lomholt, Brit. J. J. Derm., 1948, 60, 132

Intramuscular injections of 600,000 units twice weekly, or 150,000 units daily **by mouth** in 28 cases. In 20 cases of lupus improvement was observed in 3 to 6 weeks, often preceded by a **flare-up** of the condition. In some cases the addition of local therapy hastened the progress. Fourteen patients were discharged free from active lupus. In 2 cases of obstinate, cervical adenitis results were pleasing, after an acute **preliminary flare-up.** Toxicity, usually mild, were present in 50% of cases. – D.E. Macrae, Lancet, i/1947, 135.

Since **lupus vulgaris** is a **relatively harmless** disease amenable to simple lines of treatment, calciferol in **massive doses** should only be uses in selective cases under **strict supervision.** – J.T. Ingram et al., Brit. J. Derm., 1948, 60, 159.

A daily dose of 4-5 mg. (180,000 units) of calciferol was given for 3 weeks to 284 patients with **lupus vulgaris** at the **Finsen Institute**, Copenhagen; thereafter this was adjusted to individual tolerance. Treatment was continued until there was **clinical and pathological evidence of cure for at least a year,** or until a total dose of not less than 1 g. of calciferol has been given; most patients required 600 to 600 mg. The patient were kept **under observation for an average of 5 years.** Of 271 patients who completed the course **(78.5%) became symptom - free.** At the end of the observation period, 120 (42.25%) had relapsed , 83 (29.25%) remained free of disease, and 20 (7%) were lost to follow-up. Treatment of relapsed patients were **increasingly less effective.** After a second course 45.5% of patients became symptom-free, and after a third course only 30.4%. The relapse rate was high, and an increasing number of patients showed signs of intolerance. Calciferol was contraindicated in the cases of erythema induratum and in pulmonary tuberculosis. – P.V. Marcussen, Dan med. Bull., 1955, 2, 129.

Calciferol by intramuscular injection is a better mode of treatment than calciferol in tablet form for the following reasons: (1) results are more rapid; (2) pigmentation is absent; (3) there are no toxic symptoms; (4) there is little or no hypercalcemia; (5) all patients do not get a packed red-cell volume; (6) the blood urea is raised in a smaller proportion of cases. Injections of 600,000 units were given 3 times weekly for the first 3 weeks and then twice weekly. Kidney function was impaired in all patients treated with calciferol for a considerable time; whether by injection or by mouth, and **treatment should not last longer than 4 months without a rest period.** – T. Lightbound, Lancet, ii/1948, 1010.

Combined treatment (in 7 cases) with **calciferol and streptomycin** was so effective as to suggest the 2 drugs are of benefit, usually **from 5 to 12 months.** Streptomycin, 1g. Daily intramusculatly in divided doses every 4 hours, was then used in combination with the calciferol until **the lesions appeared to be inactive;** this required from 6 to 9 weeks. A striking feature, besides the **rapid and uneventful healing of the lesions,** was the thin even atrophic character of the scars, which were relatively inconspicuous. – T. Cornbleet, J. Amer. Med. Ass., 1948, 138, 1150.

PULMONARY TUBERCULOSIS. Dosage varied from 500,000 to 3,000,000 units, and length of treatment was from 20-50 days. Initially 25,000 was given with 3 mg. of vitamin B1 daily, increasing to 100,000 units daily. Of 21 patients treated, none showed significant improvement in the lung condition. – P.J. Feeny, et al., Lancet, i/1947, 438. R.W. Carslaw, ibid., 616.

ECZEMA AND NEURODERMATITIS. Satisfactory clinical results were obtained in 15 cases of resistant or chronic relapsing excema and neurodermatitis by administration of large doses of vitamin D2. Cholesterol levels, usually found to be increased before treatment became normal during healing of the skin lesions. – W. Ludwig, Hautarzt, 1953, 4, 524, per Abstr. World Med., 1954, 15, 428.

In 88 cases of **eczema remarkably rapid regression condition of the acute inflammatory condition was obtained** with 6 intravenous injections of 15 mg. of vitamin D hydrosol (Vi-De-Hydrosol, preparation of calciferol in aqueous solution) at intervals of 1 to 2 or at the most 3 days. The hydrosol must be **injected very slowly** to avoid side effects characterized by flushing of the face, dyspnea, and **afeeling of constriction and anxiety.** - A. Schnitzer, Dermatologica, Basel, 1954, 108, 332.

TUBERCULOUS GLANDS. In 5 cases tuberculous glands were treated with calciferol 50,000 units daily. The observation suggested that **calciferol in high dosage may be beneficial in tuberculous conditions other than lupus vulgaris.** – H. J. Wallace, Lancet, ii/1946, 88.

Tuberculous manifestations of slow evolution – adentitis, tenosynovitis, lupus and diseases in the **small joints** – without fever and of hyperplastic type are most likely to respond favourably. The average daily dose (in tablets) for an adult is 100,000 units daily, though during the first few months of treatment the dosage should be larger. – G. B. Dowling, Brit. J. Derm., 1948, 60, 137.

Bibliography (Section 3)

(1) The Peoples Common Sense Medical Advisor, R.V. Pierce, MD, 98th Edition, World's Dispensary Medical Association, Copyright Canada 1914, revised 1926
(2) Taber's Cyclopedic Medical Dictionary, F. A. Davis Company, 17th Edition, USA, 1993 (p 1996)
(3) Steadman's Medical Dictionary, Thomas Lathrop Steadman, A.M., M.D., 12th Revised Edition, Williams and Wilkins, England, 1933-34
(4) The Merck Manual, 12 Edition, Merck & Co. Inc, 1972 (pp 1043-1046) REDACTED
(5) The Extra Pharmacopia, Martindale, Vol 1, 24th Edition, London, The Pharmaceutical Press, 1958 (pp 319-323) REDACTED

This book has been edited by ***Shankar Shastri****, a Corporate Trainer in Communication Skills and a Faculty of ICSE English with a well-known tutorial in Mumbai. He has been a top trainer and has trained about 2000 students in Spoken English with* ***THE PERSONALITY SCHOOL by GAUTAM GARRY GUPTAA, Mumbai.***

For Corporate Seminars, Webinars and Other Information, you can email the author Deepak Kumar Gupta
at garygucci2000@hotmail.com

To speak to the author regarding any concerns you can reach him on +91 9821123216

www.ingramcontent.com/pod-product-compliance
Lightning Source LLC
La Vergne TN
LVHW091222150826
845673LV00003B/974

* 9 7 9 8 8 9 3 2 2 7 4 8 2 *